How Strong Is an Ant?

AND OTHER QUESTIONS ABOUT . . .

Bugs and Insects

STERLING CHILDREN'S BOOKS
New York

STERLING CHILDREN'S BOOKS
New York

An Imprint of Sterling Publishing
387 Park Avenue South
New York, NY 10016

Text © 2014 by Mary Kay Carson
Illustrations © 2014 by Sterling Publishing Co, Inc.

Photo credits: 8 (top left): iStockphoto © Antagain; 8 (top center): © arlindo71; 8 (top right): © Gloda;
8 (bottom left): © Okea; 8 (center): Shutterstock © Chris Howey; 8 (bottom right): © pigphoto;
13: Corbis © Jonn/Jonhér Images; 26: Getty Images © ER Degginger/Photo Researchers; 30: © yanikap.

ISBN 978-1-4549-0684-1 [hardcover]
ISBN 978-1-4549-0685-8 [paperback]

Library of Congress Cataloging-in-Publication Data
Carson, Mary Kay, author.
    How strong is an ant? : and other questions about bugs and insects / Mary Kay Carson.
        pages cm. -- (Good question)
        Audience: 6+
    Audience: K to grade 3.
    Includes bibliographical references and index.
    ISBN 978-1-4549-0684-1 (hardcover) -- ISBN 978-1-4549-0685-8 (pbk.) 1. Insects--Miscellanea--Juvenile literature.
2. Children's questions and answers. I. Title. II. Series: Good question!
    QL467.2.C3785 2014
    595.702--dc23

                                                                                                    2013045734

Distributed in Canada by Sterling Publishing
c/o Canadian Manda Group, 165 Dufferin Street
Toronto, Ontario, Canada M6K 3H6
Distributed in the United Kingdom by GMC Distribution Services
Castle Place, 166 High Street, Lewes, East Sussex, England BN7 1XU
Distributed in Australia by Capricorn Link (Australia) Pty. Ltd.
P.O. Box 704, Windsor, NSW 2756, Australia

Design by Ellen Duda
Art by Carol Schwartz

For information about custom editions, special sales, and premium and corporate purchases, please contact Sterling Special Sales
at 800-805-5489 or specialsales@sterlingpublishing.com.

Manufactured in China
Lot #:
2 4 6 8 10 9 7 5 3 1
04/14

www.sterlingpublishing.com/kids

CONTENTS

Are there more insects than people on Earth?

Small, six-legged creatures rule our planet! Insects are everywhere. They live in hot deserts and on cold mountaintops. You can find them underground, high up in the air, and in water, too. Bees, ants, wasps, butterflies, beetles, grasshoppers, flies, and other insects come in more than a million different kinds, or species. Three-quarters of all named land animals today are a type of insect.

No matter how you do the math, insects outnumber humans. In some places, there are more insects living on a single square mile than there are people on the planet. About seven billion humans live on Earth, compared to ten billion trillion or so insects. Who weighs more? People may be bigger than beetles and flies, but insects have us beat there, too. Imagine adding up the weight of every insect and every person alive today. Insects would weigh three hundred times as much as all the people.

Why are there so many insects? Being small is one survival secret. A cockroach can get by on crumbs and needs only a crack or corner to live in. Insects also have lots of offspring. A housefly lives just a few weeks but can lay a thousand eggs before dying. Wings are part of insect success, too. Most insects can fly, which helps them escape enemies and find food, homes, and mates.

How many legs does a bee have?

Insects have a really terrific body design. Their basic body structure is a big reason why there are so many insects living all over the world. It all starts with a protective shell. Think of a ladybug. That red-and-black shiny shell keeps its insides safe, like armor. Insects have no bones. They are invertebrates—animals without backbones, like worms, clams, snails, and bugs. The skeleton of an insect isn't made of bones inside its body, as yours is. A beetle's skeleton is its hard outer covering, called an exoskeleton. An insect's exoskeleton, including its legs, is made of a tough but flexible material called chitin. You walk and move thanks to muscles attached to bones. An insect's muscles attach to its exoskeleton.

Think of all the kinds, shapes, colors, and sizes of insects around the world. Incredible as it seems, ants, butterflies, and fleas share the same body plan. All adult insects have six legs and a body separated into three parts: head, thorax, and abdomen. The head is home to two huge eyes, a mouth, and antennae that both feel and smell. Most insects have two antennae between their eyes. Sandwiched in the middle of the body is the thorax. This body part includes the three pairs of legs and usually one or two pairs of wings. The body part on the end of an insect is its abdomen. Like your own belly, its abdomen is where food is digested. As well as the gut, an insect's abdomen also has equipment for getting rid of wastes, mating, and laying eggs.

Fly *

Diving Beetle *

Centipede

Scorpion

Red Knee Tarantula

Oleander Hawk Moth *

Pill Bug

* = Insect

Are all bugs insects?

While all insects are bugs, not all bugs are insects. Why not? To scientists, the word *insect* means something specific. Insects are a particular group of invertebrate animals with six legs. The word *bug*, on the other hand, doesn't really have an exact meaning. Everything from germs to crawdads can be called bugs, but that doesn't make them insects.

What bugs aren't insects? Spiders are commonly confused with insects. But a closer look gives them away. Spiders have eight legs, only two body parts, and no antennae. Ticks, eight-legged cousins of spiders, are also often mistaken as insects. Pill bugs are small bugs that roll into balls and live in damp places like basements and under rocks. Whether you call them roly polys, woodlice, armadillo bugs, or potato bugs, they are not insects. Pill bugs are actually land-living relatives of lobsters, crabs, and shrimp. Millipedes and centipedes can have hundreds of legs—way too many to be insects. The word *millipede* means "a thousand feet"! Counting legs is the best way to tell if a bug is an insect. Six is the magic number to identify an insect.

How do insects grow?

nsects aren't born looking like their parents. The young and adult forms of some insects are so unalike that they have different names: caterpillar and butterfly, woolly bear and tiger moth, maggot and housefly, or hellgrammite and dobsonfly. The process of a body changing form during growth is called *metamorphosis*. All insect life cycles include metamorphosis on the journey from egg to adult. Each separate body form is suited for one stage of the insect's life—either growing, resting, or reproducing. But not all insects develop the same way, nor do they have the same stages. There are two basic types of insect metamorphosis: complete and incomplete.

Complete metamorphosis is how moths, butterflies, ants, bees, flies, and beetles (shown below) become adults. These insects go through four separate life stages: egg, larva, pupa, and adult.

Complete Metamorphosis

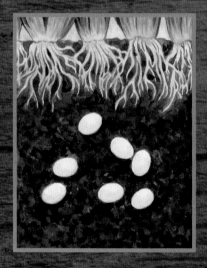

Egg

Larva

Pupa

Adult

After one of these insects hatches from its egg, it enters the larva stage as a worm–like creature. This is its eating and growing period. Some insects only eat as larvae. Once it's finished growing, a larva forms a chubby pupa. During this resting stage its entire body is rearranged and remade. Pupae are often protected by nests or thin, shell-like cases they build, including cocoons. The adult insect is what leaves the pupa's nest. It has six legs, a head, a thorax, and an abdomen. The adult is the reproducing stage.

Incomplete metamorphosis is how grasshoppers, dragonflies, cockroaches, and cicadas (shown below) become adults. They have just three stages: egg, nymph, and adult. A nymph is what hatches out of a cricket or roach egg. Nymphs often look like miniature wingless versions of the adult. The nymph stage is for eating and growing. Each time a nymph sheds its exoskeleton, or molts, it gets bigger and more like an adult. Wing buds appear after a number of molts, and with a final shed, an adult with working wings emerges ready to reproduce.

Incomplete Metamorphosis

Egg

Nymph

Adult

Where do insects live?

Insects can be found on every one of Earth's continents. Beetles are at home in hot tropical rainforests and cold mountain streams. There are even kinds of fly larvae that live in pools of crude oil, eating other insects that tumble in. Oceans are the exceptions. Few insects thrive in salty seawater.

Many insects spend their lives simply hanging out in grass, under a rock, or stuffed under bark. The fanciest homes in the insect world are built by social insects, like ants, termites, hornets, and honeybees. Social insects live together in a shared nest, or colony, like a beehive or termite mound. Not all of a colony's individual bees or ants live the same type of life. Members look different from one another and are born to do specific jobs. Huge, car-size termite mounds in Africa are built by generations of small worker termites. Larger soldier termites protect the mound but never carry mouthfuls of dirt to build it. Queens are the only termites that can lay eggs. Termite queens can live fifty years, longer than any other insect.

Queen ants or bees must sometimes start a new nest. A queen hornet chews wood into pulp and then spreads it out, letting it dry into paper. Once she's built a few cells with the paper, the queen lays eggs in them. The workers that hatch out then take over the nest-building. Honeybees build cells out of wax, not paper or mud. Beeswax is made in the bodies of worker bees. As the wax comes out, the workers shape it into six-sided cells that form honeycomb. Honeybees fill the cells with food for winter—honey. Altogether, the worker bees of a hive travel about 55,000 miles, or 88,514 kilometers (km), and visit more than two million flowers to make a single pound of honey!

Honeybees live together in a hive. Female worker bees like these collect nectar, make honeycomb and honey, and also care for larvae.

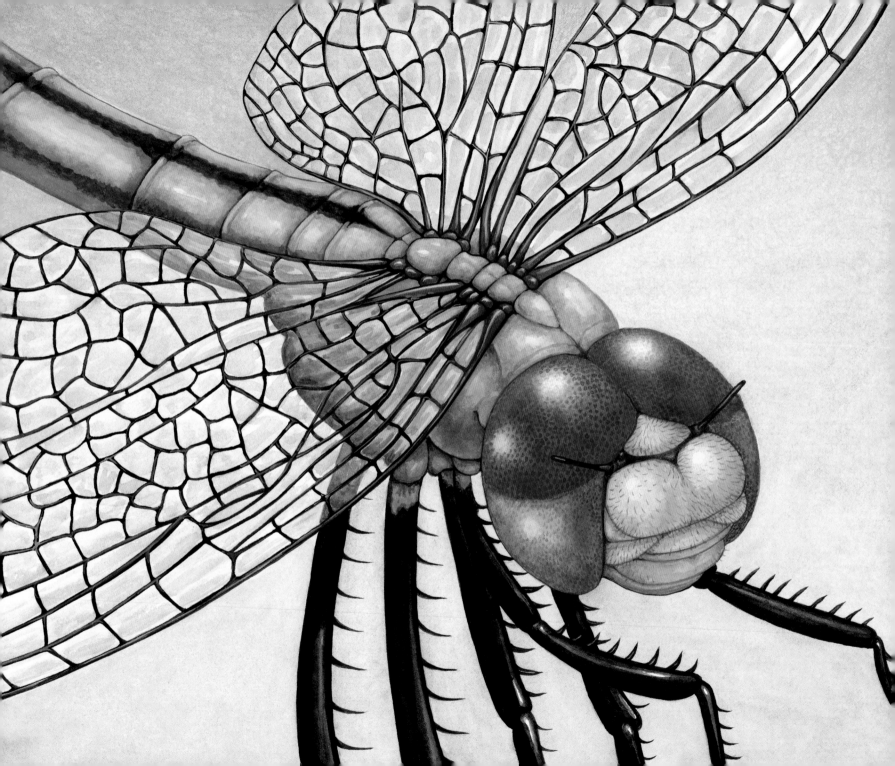

Can dragonflies see in all directions at the same time?

The world looks very different through the eyes of an insect. Most adult insects have a pair of huge compound eyes. Clusters of little lenses, called facets, make up a compound eye. Each facet captures a small part of what's in the insect's view. Together the parts make up a whole, like a picture made of dots or pixels on a screen. The number of facets varies from insect to insect. A dragonfly has the most. Its two eyes cover nearly all of its head, and each eye has up to thirty thousand facets. This means a dragonfly can see in all directions all the time. Most insects can also see ultraviolet light, which is invisible to humans.

An insect ear is similar to your eardrum. It's a thin, flat membrane that vibrates when sound strikes it. Unlike you, insects never have ears on their heads. The ears of many moths and locusts are on the sides of their bodies. Crickets and some grasshoppers have ears on their legs. While not all insects have ears, nearly all insects can hear. Most detect sound through tiny vibrating hairs on their antennae or elsewhere on their body. Caterpillars have sound-detecting hairs all over, while cockroaches hear with hairs on the end of their abdomens.

Can butterflies taste with their feet?

Antennae gather lots of information for insects. These two stalk-like structures on an insect's head allow it to smell and feel what's around it. One reason a fly is so hard to catch is that even a faint breeze moves sensitive hairs on its antennae. By the time your hand is anywhere close, the fly has felt it and flown off. Antennae also pick up smells and help insects recognize colony members and find food or mates. A male moth can smell a female moth that's up to seven miles (11 km) away.

Tasting is another important sense for insects. Many can tell if something's sweet, sour, salty, or bitter with their mouth. But ants and wasps taste by touching food and other things with their movable antennae. Honeybees and butterflies taste while they walk. Tastebuds on their feet tell them if what's underfoot is worth eating. Butterflies eat sweet nectar and can taste minute amounts of sugar. Would a bucket of water with a spoonful of sugar mixed in it taste sweet to you? It does to a butterfly.

Why do crickets chirp?

Flies buzz, bees hum, mosquitoes whine, dragonflies drone, and cicadas chirr. Insects make a bunch of different sounds—and in many different ways. The buzzing sound of wasps, dragonflies, mosquitoes, and houseflies comes from their fast-beating wings. Other insects make noise by rubbing body parts together, like legs and wings. Some grasshoppers rub a hind leg against a forewing, as if they were playing a violin. Still others create sound by scraping together their tough front wings. One of the loudest insects is the male cicada. His muscles vibrate two miniature noise–making membranes on the abdomen. Some cicada songs are loud enough to harm your hearing. Male crickets make their cheerful chirping sound by quickly running the top of one wing along the comb-like teeth at the bottom of the other wing.

Many insects buzz and chirp to attract and find mates. It's a way for the insect to let others know who and where it is. Insects communicate in other ways besides sound. Fireflies use flashes of light to attract mates. Honeybees tell others in the hive where to find food by doing a dance that gives directions. Smells are the language spoken by many insects, including army ants, which follow each other along scent trails, and moths, which use smell to find mates in the dark of night.

Do termites really eat wood?

You name it, there's likely an insect that eats it—including wood! Every plant part is a meal to one kind of insect or another. There are caterpillars that munch leaves, bark-boring weevils, sap-sucking beetles, and fruit-devouring flies. Other insects prefer meat to vegetation. Ladybugs, mantids, dragonflies, and antlions hunt and eat other insects. Dead animals, manure, and blood are also food for insects. Even things you might not consider food are edible to insects. Like what? Paper, carpet, glue, clothing, and wood. Part of the reason that there are so many different species of insects around the world is that they've adapted to eat just about anything. The secret is in their mouths.

Termites have strong wood-chomping jaws. Special gut bacteria help them digest the wood, too. The mouths of grasshoppers are for chewing leaves. Their jaws cut like scissors and also grind and crush. Moths and butterflies have tube-like mouths that reach into flowers and suck up nectar. When they're not eating, their long mouth coils up like a hose. Housefly mouths are like sponges, sopping up food. The needle-like mouths of mosquitoes pierce skin to suck blood or plant stems to drink sap. Whatever it eats, each kind of insect has developed the perfect mouth for the job.

Termites eat dead trees and things made of wood, including homes.

Can all insects fly?

Flying is a rare skill. Bats and birds do it, but the only invertebrate flyers are insects. Nearly all insects have wings and can fly. Which don't? Fleas and lice are wingless, as are primitive springtails and silverfish. Most other insects have one or two pairs of wings and fly, though some are much better at it than others. Dragonflies are fantastic fliers that can hover and turn quickly. Their thin, long bodies cut through the air like an arrow. Australia's southern giant darner dragonfly breaks the insect flight speed record at 60 miles (97 km) per hour. Dragonflies are aerial predators that put on speed to hunt down other flying insects. Dragonflies can also go the distance. Globe skimmer dragonflies cross the Indian Ocean during spring and fall migration. The twice-a-year trip is more than 11,000 miles (17,700 km) long. Butterflies can also be marathon migrators. Some of North America's monarch butterflies migrate south in the fall all the way to warmer Mexico.

How strong is an ant?

Watching a line of ants haul away crumbs bigger than themselves is an impressive sight. Some ants can lift, carry, and drag as much as one hundred times their own weight. That'd be like you lifting a car! Ants put their power to work for their colony. Each worker and soldier, queen and male, does its particular job for the good of all. Insect experts, called entomologists, have identified more than twelve thousand ant species—and keep finding more. Tropical forests are especially ant-filled places. Harvester ants build spiral-shaped mounds in India, and army ants march by the thousands through Africa's jungles. In the rainforests of Central and South America there are even ants that garden underground. Leaf-cutter ants grow and eat fungus. Worker leaf-cutter ants chew out chunks of leaves from trees and plants. Once a leaf piece is cut, a worker carries it back to the colony. Down in the nest, workers chew the leaf bits into pulp and grow fungus on it.

A colony of leaf-cutter ants dices up and hauls off all the leaves in an entire grove of fruit trees overnight. But ants aren't the strongest insects out there. That title goes to a kind of horned dung beetle called the taurus scarab. This small black beetle can pull more than a thousand times its own body weight. That's like an average adult human pulling six double-decker buses full of passengers.

Leaf-cutter ants collect leaves for their underground fungus farms.

Goliath beetles are among Earth's largest living insects. You could barely hold this one in your hand.

What is the biggest insect?

Insects used to be bigger. The biggest bugs lived before the dinosaurs about three hundred million years ago. The giants included flying predator griffinflies with 2.5-foot, or 76-centimeter (cm), wingspans and ants the size of mice. What happened to those giant bugs? The air changed. The atmosphere ancient insects breathed had more oxygen than today's air. Insects don't have lungs. A system of holes and tubes takes oxygen into their bodies. After an insect reached a certain size, the amount of air-delivering tubes needed would have to be larger than the body itself. But when the atmosphere was richer, insects didn't need as much air to get enough oxygen, so they could be bigger.

The largest insects living today come in a number of oversize shapes. Giant walking sticks are the longest insects, with skinny bodies that can stretch out to 2 feet (61 cm) in length. The largest is arguably the 6-inch (15-cm) titan beetle of the Amazon rainforest. It has jaws strong enough to snap pencils. While not as large as its titan cousin, the African goliath beetle larva is heavier, weighing in at more than 4 ounces (113 grams).

What is the smallest insect?

Most fairyflies are too small to see without a microscope. Fairyflies are actually tiny wasps, not flies. Like many kinds of wasps, they are parasites. A mother fairyfly finds the eggs of another insect and lays her eggs in them. When her egg hatches into a larva, it eats its host. The smallest species of known fairyfly lives in Costa Rica. Four of the males lined up end to end would just stretch across this printed period. The females are bigger, about a tenth of the size of a dog flea.

Fairyfly up close!

What's the deadliest insect?

Mosquitoes kill a million people each year, mostly in Africa and other tropical places. The bite itself isn't deadly. It's the diseases carried by the mosquito that kill. About fifteen hundred children die every day from the mosquito-delivered disease called malaria. Mosquito bites also spread yellow fever, dengue, West Nile, and other dangerous diseases. The sicknesses they spread make mosquitoes the deadliest of all animals, not just insects. Other biting insects—lice, fleas, flies, bedbugs—can spread diseases, too. Plagues spread by rat fleas have killed millions of people at times throughout history.

More than human health is harmed by insects. Ants, cockroaches, termites, carpet beetles, and clothes moths destroy homes and belongings.

Farmers have battled hungry insects since planting the first seeds thousands of years ago. Chemicals that kill insects, called insecticides, kill trillions of insects. Insecticides are sprayed on farm fields, gardens, and lawns. They're used in homes, buildings, and where food is stored. People use insecticides on themselves and their pets and livestock to get rid of fleas and lice. Insecticides are often dangerous chemicals. They can poison soil and water used by people and wildlife, and often kill insects besides pests.

How long do insects live?

The lifespan of an insect depends on what species it is. Some insects live decades, and others live only a few hours. Which stage of an insect's life is longest differs, too. Certain cicadas spend ten to twenty years underground as pupae but live only weeks as adults.

Entomologists study ways to stop mosquitoes from spreading diseases.

Ladybugs help farmers and gardeners by eating pesky aphids.

How do insects help people?

We all benefit from our six-legged insect friends. Honey, beeswax, silk, and dyes come from insects. Insects are food for all kinds of animals, from fish and lizards to bats and birds. People, too, are eaters of insects. Candied grasshoppers are snacks in Japan, and large moth caterpillars are harvested in many parts of southern Africa. Many plants depend on insects to deliver pollen so they can make seeds, including many of the fruits, nuts, and vegetables we eat. Everything from apples and almonds to peas and plums needs insects to grow. Insects are important recyclers, too. They help break down dead plants and animals, making nutrient-rich soil for growing plants.

The ecosystems, animals, and plants on our planet today wouldn't exist without insects. Insects were some of the first land creatures around four hundred million years ago. The earliest ancestor of all mammals, including humans, was an insect-eater that evolved soon after the dinosaurs died out sixty-five million years ago. Earth wouldn't be the same without insects.

Find Out More

Books to Read

Dussling, Jennifer. *Bugs! Bugs! Bugs!* New York: DK Publishing, 2011.

Feldman, Thea. *Insects in Action!* New York: Sterling Children's Books, 2012.

Heos, Bridget, illustrated by Stéphane Jorisch. *What to Expect When You're Expecting Larvae: A Guide for Insect Parents (and Curious Kids)*. Minneapolis, MN: Millbrook Press, 2011.

Jenkins, Steve. *The Beetle Book*. New York: Houghton Mifflin Books for Children, 2012.

Murawski, Darlyne, and Nancy Honovich. *Ultimate Bugopedia: The Most Complete Bug Reference Ever*. Des Moines, IA: National Geographic Children's Books, 2013.

Siy, Alexandra. *Bug Shots: The Good, the Bad, and the Bugly*. New York: Holiday House, 2011.

Websites to Visit*

ARTHROPODS FOR KIDS
http://kids.sandiegozoo.org/animals/insects
  The San Diego Zoo has a terrific kids' website about animals, including dung beetles, ladybugs, leaf-cutter ants, and other bugs.

BUG FACTS
www.bugfacts.net
  This site has information on North American insects, including butterflies, beetles, ants, wasps, bees, and more! There's also a checklist of common insects you can print out to keep track of your sightings.

ENTOMOLOGY FOR KIDS
http://bugs.osu.edu/Ent for Kids/entsite.html
  Pretty much everything you want to know, from insect-collecting techniques, which ones bite, and fun activities, to how to join a bug club.

*For bibliography and free activities, visit: http://www.sterlingpublishing.com/kids/good-question

Index